Be a Boss

A Guide To Earning The Trust, Respect and Loyalty Of Those Around You

By Landon T. Smith

Copyright 2017 by Landon T. Smith

Published by Make Profits Easy LLC

Profitsdaily123@aol.com

facebook.com/MakeProfitsEasy

Table of Contents

Introduction 4

Chapter 1: Like a Manager 6

Chapter 2: Tell me what it means to me 27

Chapter 3: Influential Power 52

Chapter 4: Conclusion 98

Introduction

We all want to be a boss. Not necessarily THE boss, because that simply means someone who's in charge of the workplace. We want to be A boss, that is, someone who's confident, capable and above all, earns the respect of those around him. A boss is someone who is feared and respected, loved and admired. It's easy to want to be a boss, after all, who doesn't want respect and admiration from those around him? The problem is that we often believe that in order to become a boss, we have to be charismatic, charming and slick. The idea that we need to somehow convince people to respect us through the use of cunning tricks and manipulation is a false one. There are tried and true methods to gain respect, admiration and fear, but you must be willing to develop a strong character first.

The purpose of this book is to provide a guide on how to become a boss in life. We're going to be taking a look at the concepts of respect, fear, leadership and guidance in order to garner the respect from those around you. If you've been looking for the opportunity to become a true boss, then look no further. Let's move onto the first chapter, where we will discuss the difference between a boss and a manager.

Chapter 1: Like a Manager

As stated before, everyone wants to be a boss. There is a great amount of validation and respect that comes with being the guy in charge, and life is usually better when we're running the show. Yet, many of us don't see our bosses at work as the kind of people that we aspire to be like. In fact, the running joke seems to be that our bosses tend to be sociopathic, greedy and manipulative bastards. Few people respect their bosses at work and even fewer aspire to be like their bosses.

That's because these bosses, the people who are in charge, aren't actually being a boss, they are being nothing more than managers. You see, a manager is in charge because he was given authority by someone else. He might have some kind of power, but that doesn't mean he has earned your respect. For the most part, a manager can control the people around him because he has the ability to bribe or coerce them. He can bribe them with better pay, job benefits, perks, days off or he can coerce them by threatening to fire them, docking their pay, etc.

The nature of having a manager is that their source of power doesn't come from an internal force, such as personality, likability, character, but rather it comes from an external source: carrots or sticks. Getting results through a carrot or stick approach doesn't really indicate the character or strength of an individual. Most everyone will follow a manager if he is able to sufficiently offer them external rewards, but what were to happen if your manager were to come in tomorrow and announce that the company has no more money? Most people, if not all people, would leave.

Yet, what about Pandora? The music company that is responsible for singlehandedly changing the way we listen to music ran out of money in the early days of development. Without the ability to pay their employees, the leaders stepped up and told everyone what the situation was. He was honest and asked them all to stay. And for two years, the entire Pandora team worked without a paycheck. Why? Why did they stay? Because the leader of Pandora was a boss, not a manager.

A boss has something that a manager does not: influence. At its core, leadership is influence. The difference between a boss and a manager is that a boss has the power to influence people around them, but a manager does not. The manager must use control in order to inflict his will on others, be it through a paycheck, the threat of firing or even the threat of some kind of violence. The boss uses the intangible power of influence to get people to willingly follow him, without ever having to resort to bribery or coercion in order to get that result.

In other words, a boss is someone who has the power and authority to inspire those around him to follow, without necessarily having to resort to things like money or the threat of losing a job in order to motivate him. This is the core element that separates a boss from a manager. A boss leads, a manager manages. It's simple as that.

So this means that we must first begin to come to some terms with what true leadership looks like. A lot of people get it in their heads that leadership is simply barking out orders, expecting people to follow, but once again, that is nothing more than management. No one will die for their boss, but a great many men in this world would die for a leader. So let's take a look at what the principles of true leadership are.

True Leadership Principle One: Responsibility

When the financial crisis of 2008 occurred, we saw what happens when you let a generation of managers run the show. In short, the American housing market went belly up and it took a lot of people with it, launching a recession that took nearly ten years to recover from. Yet the most common theme during this crisis was everyone saying "it's someone else's fault." The politicians blamed the bankers, the bankers blamed the investors, the investors blamed the government and so on and so forth. Tell me, how much do we respect these groups of people? How much respect does a politician, a banker or an investor command from you?

Truthfully, they don't get a lot of respect from the common person because these people almost always give up their responsibility in any crisis and point the finger at someone else. In the process, they are abdicating their control over the situation. In essence, someone who gives up his responsibility is also giving up his credibility. In times of crisis, we don't look to the people who try to pass the buck, but rather we look to the people who can accept their responsibility and offer solutions.

Someone who takes the credit for his good decision but passes off blame when he makes mistakes isn't someone to look up to. We all make mistakes, we all fail, to err is to be human. No one goes home at night and pretends that their lives are perfect, so why would people be looking to a leader who acts as if he were perfect? People who pretend that they are immaculate often transfer the blame onto others and in the act of doing so lose the respect of their peers. Someone who can own up to his choices and not point the finger at anyone else might receive heat for the decisions that he has made, but he will also receive respect.

True Leadership Principle Two: Servanthood

If we look at most examples of what passes for leadership in America, we tend to see a reoccurring pattern of people looking to their own needs and caring only about themselves. The corporate bigwigs pay themselves millions in bonuses while their company burns and people are let go left and right. The politician allows his votes to be bought by whatever corporation offers him the most amount of campaign contributions while completely ignoring the actual needs of the people. We have little respect of these false leaders because they put themselves first. Few, if any, of us would prefer to follow someone who would knowingly sacrifice us for their gain.

Truthfully, most people aren't really interested in what they can do for you, rather they are interested in what you can do for them. This doesn't necessarily mean that they want you to give them money, bribes or gifts, but rather it means that people need to know that your concern isn't making your own life better, but rather is focused on helping and caring for those around you. How many of us would follow a leader who would tell you to your face that he doesn't care anything about you and only wants you to follow him because he wants to be powerful and liked? The answer is no one. No one would follow a man who says that.

People only follow a leader when they have some vested interest in his success. And the only way a manager can transition to a boss is to adopt the mindset of being able to serve those around him. Once a person feels that they are cared about, they will begin to care about you. The phrase to describe this would be servant leadership.

A servant leader is the kind of person who uplifts and empowers his people so that they can be the best person possible. He inspires greatness and in return, those around him will begin to care deeply about him and his cause. They will respect him more and they will be motivated to go to incredible lengths to assist him in reaching his own goals, because they know they are being taken care of. Of course, servant leadership doesn't mean weakness. It doesn't mean that you have to be a doormat or that you can't discipline people or tell them what you really think. Rather, it's about the perspective that you have when you interact with others. Are you there to help them or use them? A manager uses people to achieve his own goals, but a boss helps others achieve their goals and in the process, furthers his own purposes.

True Leadership Principle Three: Position is Irrelevant

As we've mentioned before, true leadership is influence. If you want to be a great leader and someone that the people around you would consider to be a boss, then you must realize that position is irrelevant. Whether you are a janitor or a CEO of a company, your true authority lies with how you influence people. See, this is where the problems come into play. A lot of people erroneously believe that the position is the most important factor in having sway over other people, but that's only a half-truth. A position of power gives you temporary influence, but what you do with that position will indicate whether you keep your authority or whether you lose the respect of your peers.

For example, if a man were to be promoted from the position of salesman to company manager, many people would initially treat him as if he had authority. They do this out of respect or maybe fear of the position. But it is his actions that will determine how people will act towards him in the future. So he starts with a positional level of influence, but that doesn't last very long. He will have to earn the respect from other people in order to keep his positional authority. The moment that people realize that he is incompetent, a liar, a fraud or weak, he will lose his power.

A boss never allows position to hold him back. You can be someone without a job and still be respected by those around you, and if you play your cards right, you could end up with more respect than those who have high-level jobs. This might seem unrealistic to you, but think about it: if you command the respect and admiration of all of the people in your life, then it doesn't matter what your job title is. A CEO might have the admiration of respect of thousands of people, but those people won't affect his everyday life. However, the many people in your life usually have a direct impact on your quality of life.

A manager chooses to allow his position to go to his head. He thinks to himself "they have to do what I say because of my job title." While that might be true, it is a terrible way to get other people to comply with your desires, mainly because that strategy is still based on coercion and control. No one wants to follow a job position, they want to follow a living, breathing person who cares about them. The title confers nothing except an additional list of responsibilities. But how many managers look at their title as a list of responsibilities? Instead, they look at it as a means to control other people and to exert power over the weak. It is nothing short of a tragedy when a manager comes to believe that job position or title is all that matters. It matters for maybe 20 seconds, but after that, it has everything to do with *who* you are, not *what* you are.

True Leadership Principle Four: Courage

This could be the subject matter of an entire book, but alas, we do not have the time. Courage is one of the most important principles of leadership, because it allows you to live out all of the other attributes with strength and ferocity. Most managers do not have courage; they allow their fears to rule over then, as opposed to allowing those fears to fall by the wayside as they achieve greatness.

The key difference between a manager and a boss is in how they handle fear. Fear is an ever-present force that threatens to derail any plan at any moment. There are so many different kinds of fears, fears of the unknown, fears of the future, fears of failure but they all have something in common: they convey a powerful emotional burden that can crush us if we aren't careful.

Fear is the ultimate motivator, in the sense that it motivates us to the act one way or the other. Fear never causes a person to stay still, it either makes us run away from the obstacle, or it prompts us to run toward the danger. To say that we are a people who can exist without fear is to lie, for fear is a fact of human life. We cannot have courage without fear, so we must embrace the reality that fear is a necessity in order to be courageous. What we must learn to pay attention to is how fear manifests itself in our lives.

The most common manifestation of fear is in control. Most managers are deeply afraid of loss, pain, suffering or looking foolish, so in an attempt to quell their fears, they try to control other people. Such a principle is nothing more than foolishness, because as stated before, you can't really control others. So these attempts at control are things such as bribery, coercion, threats or even inflicting fear on other people so that the manager may convince himself that he is safe. But he isn't safe at all. In fact, he is only further increasing his fear by trying to inflict his will on others.

To be a leader with courage means to accept that you don't have control over everything, that fear is part of the process and it is something to move past. The boss doesn't try to control other people so that he feels better about himself, rather he allows people to act however they will, in spite of the fear of losing their control. When we allow our fear to rampage through us, it will be like a wild animal let loose in a house, it will destroy everything in its way and not even know why. To be a boss, you must have mastery over your fear.

Courage is the word we use when we talk about having mastery over our fear. If you want to be courageous, you must realize that we are not required to act on our emotions. The emotions within us are nothing more than warnings and signs telling us to be aware of certain factors. Fear is present whenever the mind feels that danger is near. These are nothing more than suggestions, however, and we are not required to follow through with them. These emotions can be powerful things, however, and the fact that we are dealing with them might lead us to feel as if we don't have a choice in the matter. Truthfully, we always have a choice. No matter how powerful your emotions are, no matter how afraid you are, you always have a choice. You can choose to act in spite of your fears and in the process, exhibit great courage. The flipside is that if you choose to indulge in your fears, you aren't really in control of yourself.

You are allowing emotions to act for you and in the process you will lose the ability to influence others. People do not want to follow someone who acts randomly, based on whatever their emotions are at the time. Instead, they are looking for people who are calm and collected, able to act under pressure without allowing their own fears to prevent them from doing anything of value.

So as you can see, there is a great difference between a manager and a boss. A boss is the kind of guy who you would go to in times of trouble, someone who you would rely on in a pinch, whereas a manager is someone who has the power to wield their authority like a club. Don't ever make the mistake of thinking that just because you are in charge of a project, a company or a job that you are somehow in control of the situation. The truth is, unless you are able to follow the four true principles of leadership, you won't have much control over anything.

With that being said, competency is only one part of being a boss. The next component is respect. Let's move onto the next chapter, where we will look at all of the moving parts that come in with commanding the respect of those around you.

Chapter 2: Tell me what it means to me

Respect. We all crave it, we all want to have it, but what exactly does it mean to be respected in this world? Does it mean that people think fond thoughts of us? Does it mean that they are willing to listen to what we have to say? What's so interesting is that most everyone will agree that it is a good thing to be respected, but few people actually understand what respect is.

There's an old phrase about respect. The saying goes "you've got to give respect in order to get it." This might be somewhat of an erroneous statement, however, because that seems to indicate that unless someone is actively respecting you, there is no reason to respect them. And since we don't have clear understandings of respect, things get even murkier for us. People tend to come to false conclusions, that in order for them to be able to respect someone else, they must be given respect first. But this creates a Mexican standoff of sorts, where two people refuse to give one another respect without receiving it from the other. So how then, do we get respect? Quite simply put, we must understand what respect *actually* means.

Respect is nothing more than admiration. This might look a little disappointing at the beginning, but let's break it down on a deep level. Admiration means more than looking at someone with stars in your eyes. What admiration translates to are three basic principles: positive relationship, deferment and protectiveness. Let's take a look at each piece.

Positive Relationship:

When someone has respect for you, it means that some aspect of their relationship with you is a positive one. This doesn't necessarily mean that you are buddies or friends, but rather they are willing to treat you as a friend instead of a foe. There have been cases of people being on opposite sides of the fence, but still able to function with kindness and love towards the other person. This is what respect means at its core, that you can be at odds, but still function in a healthy, positive relationship.

Taking things a step further, if you are able to have a positive relationship with someone who isn't at odds with you, chances are they will make your life even better. This is an important component of admiration, if someone respects you, it means that their relationship will work out in your favor.

Deferment:

Deferment is an interesting principle. It essentially involves a form of humility, or being willing to put your own opinion aside in favor of someone else. To defer to someone means that you are willing to trust their expertise or their thoughts better than your own instincts. For example, if you hire a contractor to do a job, you might not understand what their plan is, but you are willing to defer to their expertise and in the process of this deferment, you trust them to get the job done well. Deferment is trust. When you are willing to give someone the benefit of the doubt, you are showing that you trust them with the job, no matter what your feelings might be.

There is a great humility in deferment, primarily because we find our own natural instincts are to believe that we are in the right. The only way we can truly defer is to learn how to ignore those feelings that tell us we are the ones who are correct on the subject matter. To defeat the ego is to learn how to defer.

Protectiveness:

Part of respect is the willingness to step up and defend the one that you admire. You can protect their reputation by refusing to speak negatively about them, you can protect them in business by making sure that no one tries to take advantage of them, and in some circles, you could even end up physically protecting them. We become protective of the people that we admire, there is no getting around this. Respect often confers a willingness to step up and watch over the interests of our allies.

These three elements are essentially what makes up respect. There are, of course, dozens of other benefits to respect, but these are the core of admiration and as such, are the core of what it means when someone shows you respect in your life. Now, if we were to look at the adage again, "you've got to give respect to get it," does it still make sense? All three of these things, deferment, protectiveness and a positive relationship are a *response* to the actions of someone. We don't build positive relationships in order to receive them, we don't defer to people in order to receive deferment, instead these are the natural results of a strong connection between two people.

And in the word connection, we find the reality of respect. Respect doesn't come from a trade, but rather from a personal connection that causes us to admire the other person. This changes the nature of respect from being a constant standoff between two people who demand the other's respect before they give it over, to instead being one where two individuals are working together to build a strong personal relationship. The stronger the connection that two people have, the more natural these three responses will occur. And that means, the two people will begin to develop respect for one another.

Now, here is where it gets even more interesting. You don't necessarily have to have respect for a person in order to gain their respect. You just have to have a personal connection in which they feel that they are trusted, cared for and watched over. This means that respect isn't necessarily always a two-way street. You can garner respect of someone who you don't feel is very respectable, but you must still have some kind of personal connection with them. In other words, you must have influence over them in order to build that connection. Which brings us to the next part in the quest to gain respect: Credibility.

What does the word credibility mean to you? Credibility is just as necessary of a component of respect as admiration is. Credibility means that people believe what you say. Credibility, in fact, can be broken down into three distinct pieces: word, deed and reputation. Let's take a look at each one of these elements in detail.

Word:

Have you ever met someone who seems to always be slinging tall tales, the kind of the stories that sound like a lot of fun but don't seem quite right? How about someone who you know to be a chronic liar, always telling half-truths in order to make themselves seem interesting? The words that we use are extremely important, because people tend to remember what we say. Not only do they remember what we say, they also are ready to use our own words against us at a moment's notice.

Someone who is always lying, or who constantly flatters others in the hopes of controlling them, will never truly be able to have credibility, because people will always be suspicious of him or her. The words that we use are extremely valuable and we should be cautious not to be too quick to speak, or worse, speak falsely with others. While there are many different elements to credibility, there is one principle that stays the same no matter what: it can take a lifetime to gain credibility, but a few seconds to lose it entirely.

So what is the difference between credible words and words that have no credibility? Truthfully, it comes down to intent. The difference between gratitude and flattery often lies in the intent of the person saying the words. A flatterer is looking to gain something; someone who's complimenting in earnest isn't looking for anything other than to express emotions of thankfulness or joy. The liar looks to make himself look good and important. The truthful man would speak truth even when it would be to his detriment. This creates a great level of credibility, however, because it shows that the man is more concerned with being truthful than preserving himself.

A manager is the kind of guy who would lie whenever it would be convenient for him. After all, the most important thing in the world is how people perceive him, so he is looking to always protect himself through words. A boss isn't concerned about mere appearances and would rather people look at him with respect and admiration, and as such, he keeps true to his words.

Deed:

Words are a valuable component of credibility, but they aren't the only part of it. In fact, words are simply the foundation of credibility, but they alone don't do much. How many of us know people who are always talking about their big plans, but never do them? Or talk to individuals who make promises and oaths, but never keep them? In reality, a boss doesn't live off of words alone, because words don't do much to change the universe around them. The ancient Romans had a phrase, facta, non verba, which means deeds, not words. No matter how much you talk about something, if you don't actually act when the time is right or necessary, people won't take you seriously. This is a fact about reality. The people who get stuff done automatically have credibility in the world.

Think about the old adage "don't take financial advice from someone who's broke." Simple enough, right? If you don't have the actions to back up what you are saying to people, they will never take you seriously. So what does this mean for someone who wants to be a boss? It simply means that you must always be willing to back up your words with your deeds and people should be able to clearly see that you are an individual who gets stuff done. In doing so, you will increase your credibility by a high amount and people will naturally trust you more. And the more they trust you, the more you will be able to influence those around you.

Reputation:

The final building block in the credibility spectrum is reputation. Now, reputation is an interesting beast, because it is something that you don't have total control over. Reputations are fickle things and they can change in a moment's notice. One minute you could be considered to be an upstanding member of society and the next your name could be all over the news. There are aspects to our reputation that we can control, such as our behavior and how we act, but there are also aspects that we simply cannot, such as what other people are saying about us.

It would be a fool's errand to try and get everyone else in the world to talk about us in a positive light, so that isn't the purpose of this section. Rather, the point is to highlight how you should guard your reputation very carefully. There are things that you can do to insulate yourself from the various traps and trials that can steal away your reputation. Let's take a look at some of them.

Reputation Keeper One: Take it easy on Social Media

It is fascinating how even the most dignified individuals can end up looking like raving lunatics on social media. The way the internet is wired, a single controversial statement can put you all over the newswires in less than ten minutes of you sending out the Facebook message or Tweet. If you want a simple example of how a nobody quickly becomes an international sensation in the span of only a few hours, look no further than Justine Sacco. Justine was a PR consultant with barely any followers on twitter, about 170 people total. She tweeted a joke that was incredibly tasteless and even racist sounding, and while she was aboard a plane, news of her words caught fire. All it took was for one follower to retweet her post for thousands of people to start talking about her and her controversial words. In the process of this entire event, she was blissfully unaware of her status as a new controversial figure since her phone couldn't connect to the internet at the time. By the time her plane landed, she was in serious trouble. Eventually, she lost her job and her name typed into Google will forever bring up reminders of her words.

So you must be willing to keep your activity on social media in check, because you never know who is watching. Resist the urge to type up controversial opinions, repeat jokes that could be offensive and always make sure to treat one another with civility and respect. If you give into the temptation to say something potentially damaging on the internet, no matter how quickly you delete it, there is a huge chance someone has taken a screen shot of it. Follow this simple rule to keep your reputation in check at all times: **assume everything that you put on the internet will be there forever.** This assumption will save your life.

Reputation Keeper Two: Learn to walk away

Emotions are a powerful thing. When we are in emotional moments, we feel a powerful surge run through us that tells us that we must act a certain way. Sadness can cause us to weep, anger can cause us to rage, all of these feelings will lead us to a place of severity if we aren't careful. The problem is that when it comes to the more powerful emotions, such as anger, we can often find ourselves in places of real temptation to act in a manner that is most unbecoming of us. The problem is that when we give into our emotions, we might do something that we can never take back. There is a moment when you cross from emotion to action, and when you cross that bridge, you are condemning yourself to living a life that will *forever* be affected by those actions.

Therefore, it is most important for you to learn how to control yourself in spite of your emotions at all times. The consequences of letting your emotions get the best of you, even for a few moments, can cost you everything. Let's look at a person who's actions made him very famous for a brief period of time, a man by the name of Steven Slater. Slater, in 2010, was a flight attendant aboard a Jet Blue plane that was parked on the runway. He was having some difficulty with a passenger, leading him to snap and announced over the speaker system that he quit. He then grabbed two beers and went over to the emergency evacuation slide, deployed it and slid out of the plane.

Initially, the American media cheered for this guy, because he represented the spirit of the worker who was oppressed. Finally, everyone said to themselves, a guy who was willing to stick it to the man and go out on his own terms. In a lot of ways, he became a folk hero, but only for a short amount of time. You see, what a lot of people don't know about those inflatable evacuation slides is that they deploy with a significantly high amount of force, after all, they are designed to help people escape a plane in the case of an emergency. The speed and velocity of these slides could actually kill a person! And during the time that the plane was on the runway, there were quite a bit of people around the airplane, preparing it for launch. In other words, Slater's emotions got the best of him and he ended up endangering the lives of those around him just because he was frustrated. His reward at first looked like immense popularity, but as the public began to learn about the dangers of his actions and the recklessness of his choices, it began to turn. To make matters worse, Slater ended up being brought up on felony charges for criminal misdemeanor and ended up owing ten thousand dollars to JetBlue for his choice. A moment, hardly 5 minutes of action, led to a lifetime of him trying to recover his reputation and deal with the consequences of his actions. The lesson here? Don't let your emotions get the better of you, your reputation can't afford it.

Reputation Keeper Three: Don't backbite

Backbiting is the perfect phrase to explain what it means when you are talking bad about someone behind their back. A backbiter is someone who waits until his friends or neighbors aren't present to sink his teeth into them, when they are unable to defend themselves. There is nothing wrong with airing complaints with others and getting into arguments with people, provided that they are around to have the discussion, but if you are talking ill about someone without them hearing you, you're essentially unfairly fighting against someone.

Backbiting creates a very negative reputation about you. The interesting thing about speaking ill about others behind their back, is that most people will be happy to listen to you talk about the person that you don't like. They might even be willing to join in, but your reputation will weaken in their eyes and they won't trust you. Worse yet, they're probably talking poorly about you behind your back.

In an office environment, this can be downright dangerous. Office politics can easily lead you to make poor decisions in speaking badly about others in order to score political points with your coworkers, but in doing so, you are damaging your credibility. Everyone likes to listen to a gossip, but no one respects one.

When you combine credibility with admiration, you get respect. Not only do people like you and have positive relationships with you, they also know that you are someone they can trust. This will increase your influence with those around you on a passive level. But what are you to do if you already have a solid base of respectability, but you don't have quite the influence that a boss would have? Well, let's move over to the next chapter and take a look.

Chapter 3: Influential Power

Influence, as we've stressed throughout this book, is the key to becoming a boss. When you're a boss, you are able to get people to follow after you, listen to you, respect you and most importantly, act on your behalf. There are a great many ways to build up passive influence with those around you, but after a while, you start to reach a point where you might want to increase your influence even more. What else can you do after you have worked to gain credibility, earned the admiration of others and you are still lacking in a sense of confidence and strength? Quite simply, you must begin to develop certain practices and habits that will actively increase your influence with others. Let's take a look at a list of the different aspects that make up a boss.

Aspect One: Image

Image refers to how people perceive you. There are quite a few components that make up your image, and if you neglect to take care of these areas, you might end up realizing that you don't necessarily garner the command and respect of those around you. Now, there are intangible pieces of image, such as reputation, but that's not what we're talking about here. We're talking more about how you physically look.

Perhaps one of the greatest tragedies in all of the world is that people do indeed judge others by how they look. While we would all prefer to be judged by the content of our character rather than our external appearances, we don't have the luxury to enforce others to see things our way. People tend to make snap judgments based off of how others look and there will never really be any changing of this. When we are forced to confront this fact, we have two choices. We can live in spite of this, or we can adapt to it. By living in spite of it, you aren't going to be building much respect because people will always be judging you off of the first impression. No one looks at a schlub and says "that person is a boss."

Therefore, if you are serious about gaining the admiration and respect of those in your life, you must be willing to focus on improving your image. Now, let's not go crazy here, we aren't saying that in order for you to gain respect that you must be so focused on image that you fundamentally change yourself, but rather you take care of yourself to a degree that is reasonable.

So what does reasonable look like? In general, we would talk about what you wear. It is true that clothing can really make or break you when it comes to making first impressions. Let's take a look at the four elements of physical appearance and what you can do to improve upon them.

Appearance Element One: Grooming

Simple enough, how you take care of your hygiene determine what people will think of you for a variety of reasons, mainly because hygiene is the one thing that is most noticeable when it is absent. Someone who has body odor, poorly groomed nails, a scruffy appearance tends to convey to people the phrase "I don't care." More so, if your odor is strong enough, it can convey to people "I don't want to be around you."

Few folks enjoy being around someone who has abysmal hygiene routines and the failure to groom oneself sufficiently can be very destructive when it comes to building up a good rapport with others around you. Therefore, you must be willing to take care of the basics of everyday hygiene. Shaving, showering and putting on inoffensive deodorants are a must.

Some people might not deal with body odor issues, but might end up erring the other side, by choosing to wear cologne that is strong and overpowering. This can be just as bad as body odor, mainly because cologne is a very powerful substance and when it is strong enough, it can be repelling to most people.

The most efficient way to be a boss in the grooming area is to focus on building a good, strong and daily routine that allows for you to take care of the necessities each morning. This involves making sure that you start your day early enough to where you are able to spend sufficient time on the grooming routine. A lot of people these days have a habit of just rolling out of bed and going straight to work after brushing their teeth, but it's going to take a lot more if you want to have that edge over others. Building up influence takes a sufficient amount of time and part of that time must be spent on your grooming routine.

Appearance Element Two: Style

In addition to your hygiene and grooming, you must also focus on having an appropriate style of clothing. Now, we are not saying that you should become dependent on the styles of the current time period, because fashion trends are fickle, coming and going as the months and years go by. But there are principles of style that you should be willing to follow as to make the most of your appearance. These principles don't require you to necessarily purchase the most expensive or fancy clothes at all. The truth is that all you need to do is obtain clothing that fits well, is comfortable and look good on you. Avoid clothes that are old, ripped or too baggy. You don't necessarily have to focus on making sure all of the colors match perfectly, but by putting in some basic effort into building a wardrobe, you can avoid the appearance of looking ragged or ratty in front of your peers.

It might seem a little vain to be focused on dressing well, but you will see that when you begin to wear clothes that you are comfortable and stylish in, your confidence level will naturally increase. The more confident you look, the more confident you will feel. If you are skeptical, you might be surprised to find out that studies have shown that people who wear lab coats during tests perform better than those who aren't wearing them. Why is that? Mainly because those wearing the lab coats *felt* smarter because lab coats are traditionally associated with being intelligent. Clothing does have a proven effect on how we perceive ourselves as well as how others perceive us as well.

Appearance Element Three: Posture

Our physical posture affects how people perceive us on a primal level. Regardless of how advanced we become as a race, humans will always act on cues that are subconscious. The brain works very quickly and is always looking to perceive threats as well as other pertinent pieces of information. While you might not actively be thinking about it, your subconscious brain is always working to make sure that you stay as well informed as possible about your surroundings. These subconscious cues lead us to make assumptions about other people. And since our brains are rapidly processing information on a subconscious level, we have the power to influence others on that level as well. The easiest way to influence this process in other people is to work on your posture.

Our postures tell other people a lot about us. A man walking along with a slumped down head, dejected look on his face will signal to us that he is sad about something. A man with a scowl and a fast pace, fists clenched and teeth bared will indicate that he is angry or looking for trouble. The primal brain will rapidly look at physical posture as a way to inform you about what you should be feeling about the other person. And in spite of this, we often pay very little attention to how we are portraying our physical presence. And in neglecting this fact about ourselves, we could be sending a whole host of negative signals to the people around us.

Stop for a moment and ask yourself what your posture is right now. Are you leaned forward, craning your neck to read? Are you sitting up straight? How does your jaw feel, is there tension in there? Chances are, you didn't really notice how you were sitting until attention was brought to it. Then you immediately become aware of your physical presence. Yet, it's so easy to forget about how we are carrying ourselves. This is primarily because posture and physical presence is nothing more than a habit. Your brain gets used to you holding yourself a certain way and then it automates the process, making it an unconscious habit.

So, what does a good posture look like? Well, it depends on what you are trying to convey. If you want people to see that you are disarming, kind and fun, you can focus on smiling more, keeping your body calm and relaxed as well as walking with a slight rhythm. If you want to convey that you are in charge, you're going to want to keep your chest wide, back straight, chin tilted high and you want to walk with confident steps. By maintaining awareness of your body at all times, you will keep yourself from slouching or shuffling about. Each step should be intentional and confident. The more you keep a good posture, the more of a habit it will become.

Slouching is truly the enemy, and not just because it's bad for your back. Someone who slouches is signaling to others around them that they are not the alpha, but rather are the weakest in the room. It displays a lack of confidence and signals to the more predatory types of people around you that you can be taken advantage of. You can counteract this by choosing to be more intentional with the way you carry yourself.

Appearance Element Four: Voice

The element of appearance isn't something that is visible, but rather it is audible. Your voice is one of the most powerful things that you can have in your arsenal, but it can also be a detractor in your life if you aren't careful. Now, let's clear something up: you cannot really change your voice by the time that you are an adult. You don't have the power to transform the way you sound to other people, but you can control what you do with your voice. Things like volume, projection, confidence and strength are all up to you. Don't underestimate the value of your voice when you use it right.

Think about a person who stammers constantly, not due to any speech impediment but simply because they are nervous or uncomfortable. Compare that to the suave individual who is able to talk without fear and you can see there is a very obvious difference in how people use their voices. Your voice has the power to persuade, but only if you are able to unlock its potential.

How can you unlock your voice's potential? Simply put, you need to learn how to project clearly and confidently. Projection gives you the ability to sound confident, regardless of how you feel at the moment. So how can we learn to project? You just need to learn how to speak using your diaphragm. Let's try a quick exercise. Sit straight up and take a deep breath. Once you've breathed in, let out a strong exhale, and take notice of your ribcage and how it expands. That area is your diaphragm and by learning how to breathe through it, you will be able to project your voice louder than if you were just to speak normally. Projection essentially involves you speaking clearly and loud enough for people to be able to hear you.

Don't underestimate the value of what volume can do for you when you are talking to others. Volume pretty much dictates your authority level. Not only does it control how people perceive you in public speaking situations, but when you are able to project effectively, you will be able to gain the attention of plenty more people. Conversations in large groups can be a competition to get a word in edgewise and most of the time we find that if we aren't loud enough, no one will listen. It doesn't really matter what you have to say, if you don't have the strength to be heard, no one will care. So focus on developing a strong, projecting voice and use it as often as you can. The more confident you sound, the more people will respect you.

Now, after you have worked hard to maintain a good image and you've done a good job with your appearance, it's time to move onto the next aspect of building more influence: Confidence.

Aspect Two: Confidence

Confidence is one of the most essential pieces to being a boss, because it allows you to act unfettered in the face of self-doubt. One of the most toxic things that we can endure as people are the feelings of doubt, fear and anxiety that rise up within us at all times. When we see someone who is confident, we often think "Wow,

I want to be like them!" But when it's our turn to speak publicly, we feel an intense stage fright, or worse yet, we don't even try to speak.

Without confidence, you will never really be able to look like a boss in front of other people. However, most of us who are lacking in confidence don't really know how to get it. To a lot of people, confidence looks like some kind of inherited trait, you either have it or you don't. However, this belief isn't particularly true at all. Confidence isn't based on some genetic disposition or inherent superiority to other people, but rather it is based on of a few tried and true principles that if you follow, you will be able to be confident as well. Let's take a look at what these principles are:

Confidence Factor One: Internal Conversation

One of the most omnipresent things in your life is what is known as your internal conversation. The inner dialogue is always going on. There is a still small voice in your head that is always talking to you about something. Yet, for those who lack confidence, the internal conversation sounds extremely negative. This inner dialogue isn't positive or uplifting, but rather it is hostile, frustrating and above all, sabotaging your efforts. When you go to do something, your inner critic will tell you that you are going to mess up. When you begin to experiment with new things, the inner critic will sabotage your efforts by telling you that failure is the worst thing possible.

Psychologists have noted that the way we converse with ourselves will determine our confidence levels in just about whatever we are doing. If the voice is a negative one, good luck trying to ever achieve anything of value. So stop for a moment and reflect on your own inner thought life. Do you find yourself constantly being barraged by self-criticism and hostility? Do embarrassing moments haunt you? Are you anxious about the things that you said long ago? If so, you are probably the victim of a terrible inner critic.

The good news about our inner critic is that this voice is nothing more than our subconscious mind repeating thoughts that *you* have been thinking throughout your life. I would liken this to a record that repeatedly plays the same song, but you were the one to put the record on the record player. You have the power to change the song any time that you want, but you just need to be willing start thinking differently.

Our own thoughts control what we are feeling throughout the days. If you are primarily thinking negative thoughts, you won't have the confidence to achieve greatness when you desire. So you must be willing to start thinking positive thoughts as a means to counteract the inner critic. This isn't to say that positive thinking will magically change your mindset overnight, but you must realize that if you want to be more confident, you must be continuously thinking confident thoughts.

The brain is interesting in the fact that the more you think a certain way, the more it will begin to subconsciously repeat those messages. So if you are constantly telling yourself "I suck and I'll never be able to talk in front of people," your brain will soak that message up and repeat it every chance that it gets. However, if you begin to say to yourself, "I am good at public speaking and I can do so without freaking out," eventually your brain will begin to believe that message. The more you work on removing negative inner dialogue and replacing it with positive inner dialogue, the more confident you will become.

Confidence Factor Two: Perspective

There are certain things that never really change when it comes to doing things that require confidence. For example, if you're ever hoping to reach a point in your life where you are able to act with confidence and courage without your heart-rate increasing or feeling nervous, then I have some bad news for you. Those feelings don't really go away, no matter how confident you are. They are nothing more than a natural output of how we feel when we are in places of stress. Speaking up when everyone is watching you can be a very stressful situation. Taking a stand for something you believe in takes the utmost confidence and can be a nerve-wracking experience. Even the greatest actors in this world still get a little nervous when it comes to performing. Confidence doesn't mean that you don't feel those uncomfortable feelings. Confidence means that your perspective on those feelings has changed.

Think about the professional athlete who is competing in some cutting edge contest where the chance of failure is astronomically high. They often approach the competition with a coolness and confidence that allows them to perform and even win. How do they do this? They have a different perspective on the bundle of feelings and nerves that are within them. Instead of looking at the feelings of butterflies, nervousness, worry and even fear as a negative, they look at these things as a positive experience. Nervousness is just excitement, worry is concern and fear is understanding of the gravity of the competition. In other words, they are able to change their perspective on their emotions and in the process the emotions are a lot less controlling than they used to be.

Now, let's think about the areas where you lack confidence in. Chances are, your emotions are playing a big part in why you aren't confident. You might not *feel* confident when it's time for you to unveil your big business plan to a friend, but it's important for you to know exactly what those feelings are. The more you are able to identify each emotion that you are experiencing, the better you will be able to get a new perspective on them.

Try to think about what is the purpose of each emotion that you are feeling. Every emotion that we feel has a reason to exist, they are meant to serve us, not hinder us. The problem is that we generally don't know how to interpret our emotions and instead look at the overwhelming strength of them as a bad thing and so we try to run away from them. Our emotions are helpers and we must seek to understand from them.

Think about that the next time that you are in a situation where you need to be confident, but you aren't feeling like it. If you are feeling fear, sorrow, worry, anxiety or nervousness, you must stop and ask why you are feeling that way. Once you ask those hard questions, you may end up realizing that there really is nothing to be afraid of in that moment. Run a few worst case scenarios in your mind and really play them out. Try to determine what the actual worst thing that could happen in that scenario and you might end up realizing it's not such a bad ordeal after all.

Many times, the uncertainty of situations can scare us far more than we realize. The unknown is a great contributor to a lack of confidence, which brings us to the next point.

Confidence Factor Three: Experience

Experience is an unmistakably important factor when it comes to building up confidence. When we don't have the proper amount of experience, we are facing the great unknown and this can create a powerful sensation of fear. The difference between most seasoned, confident people and those who are lacking in confidence is usually experience. The fact is, the more experienced you are the more confident you will be.

So when it comes to things like public speaking, making pitches, requesting someone's help or writing a book, if you are brand new to the process, your confidence might be very low. There are some things that you can do to boost that confidence, but truthfully, nothing will boost it as much as just getting it over with anyway. Then, the next time you embark on that particular area, you will have the experience to fall back on. The more experienced you are, the less overwhelmed you will be by your emotions.

This, of course, isn't to say that you will stop feeling those bundles of emotions, because as we said before, they don't really go away. But the experience will help you feel safer than if you were to try and do it without any previous knowledge whatsoever. Let this be a lesson, then. If the only thing stopping you from moving forward on a plan that requires confidence is the lack of experience, then just suck it up and push through. The more you do something, the easier it will get each time and that is a fact.

Confidence Factor Four: Understanding Failure

The average business owner will fail a number of times before his business takes off. Athletes must endure plenty of games where they blow it colossally. Even politicians must often endure great failures if they want to reach a place of greatness. Yet, what does our society tell us about failure? Society tells us that failure is a bad thing and it should be avoided at all costs. This is a terrible thing to believe, because failure is the single most necessary ingredient if you want to become successful in this life.

Failure has the power to teach you all of the lessons that are necessary for success the next time, but only if you are willing to learn these lessons. If you look at failure as a bad thing, as something to flee from and to avoid, then you are condemning yourself to forgoing all of the good things that come out of failure. When you fail, you have the opportunity to learn how to do things better the next time. You have the opportunity to make changes, tweak the formula, learn new skills and make up for your shortcomings. In other words, there isn't much wrong with failing.

However, there is a tremendous pressure in our modern culture to get away from failure as much as possible. This creates a strange link between our performance and our confidence. When we feel that there is a possibility for failure in something, such as public speaking, we grow concerned about failing. This concern can become so overwhelming that it prevents us from being confident when we speak, as the only thing we can think about is how bad it would be to fail miserably. We get so laser focused on avoiding the bad experience of failure that we actually end up failing quite miserably. Or worse yet, we don't even try.

The confident man is the man who isn't afraid of failure. Instead, he chooses to embrace failure for all its worth. He allows it to teach him, to show him the error of his ways and he allows it to correct his behavior. When he makes mistakes, he accepts the lessons that they have to teach and grows from them. He doesn't spend the rest of his life trying to get away from failure, because his perspective is that failure is a good thing. To quote Winston Churchill on the matter:

"Success is not final, failure is not fatal: it is the courage to continue that counts." - Winston Churchill

And Churchhill was certainly the man who believed in the power of not fearing failure.

In the early days of Nazi Germany, when Hitler's forces were slowly beginning to move out and seize territory that did not belong to them, Churchhill began to denounce the Nazi's. He claimed that there was a serious danger and that Nazi Germany would soon begin to plague the entire world. No one in parliament believed him and he was somewhat of a joke to the political elite. Yet in spite of this failure to convince the people of the danger, Churchill carried on with his message and denounced Hitler with ferocity. Neville Chamberlain, the prime minister at the time, began interactions with Hitler that were less than favorable. This policy was known as appeasement, and meant that England would be allowing Hitler to take any territory he wanted from their allies, in order to spare England from Germany's wrath.

Churchill's endurance finally paid off, when he was able to win the Prime Minister position and chose to take a stand against Hitler in totality, refusing to bargain or make any deals with Nazi Germany. He stood alone against a powerful force, refusing to back down. Of course, we know the end of this story, that Churchill was able to lead England to fight against the Nazis and eventually the regime was toppled, but what allowed Churchill to lead his people to victory? Quite simply, it was the fact that he wasn't afraid to fail. And keep in mind that for a government leader, the cost of failure was very high, but he was able to move forward with confidence and oppose the evils of Hitler because he didn't allow the fear of failure to control him. Now, history holds Churchill as one of the greatest people to have ever lived because of his fierce oratorical skills and unwavering strength in the face of adversity. In other words, he was a total boss!

You have nothing to fear about failure. Despite the toll it might take, despite the personal costs that you might incur when you fail, it will ultimately do you well in the future. However, if you are so afraid of failure that you fail to act, then you will never become the confident person that you desire to be. It's a choice, you can act and possibly fail, or you can refuse to move and fail permanently. It's up to you.

Confidence Factor Five: Get Rejected

And the last piece of building up great confidence is something that is highly actionable. One of the greatest things that can hold us back when we want to be confident is the fear of being rejected. Rejection is a painful experience and most people would do anything to avoid it. Rejection leads us to question our own self-worth, our value and our meaning in life. Most people cannot handle rejection and so they try to live a life that avoids any chance of rejection.

This is unfortunate, because someone who's going to be a boss will most likely face more rejection than not. Being confident, strong and self-actualized constantly requires you to put yourself out there and face the possible wounds of rejection. But when you get hit with rejection, you might end up feeling the temptation to quit, to stop trying and to just retreat. This is problematic because if you are someone who stands for something in this life, if you're trying to achieve something, you will be rejected. This is guaranteed.

So what are we to do when we know that there is a great pain that is inevitable if we are to achieve greatness? Is there some great technique to avoid it hurting so bad? Well, actually there is! This technique is known as rejection therapy and was developed by a person who lacked total confidence in just about every area of his life. His name is Jia Jang and he decided that he was tired of being so socially afraid and awkward when it came to making requests, so he developed a method of getting over his social anxieties. He called this method rejection therapy and all he did was spend 100 days asking random people on the street with the most outlandish requests. These requests would easily be shot down by other people and would expose him to a constant stream of rejection. His theory was that the more he would be rejected, the tougher he would become and the easier it would be to bear the brunt of rejection.

Over the course of two years of this experiment, he discovered that it did indeed increase his capacity to face rejection. This is an extremely valuable lesson for us to learn: most social anxieties and fears can be overcome with a certain level of practice. If you are someone whose fear of rejection prevents you from getting the things you want out of life, then you should start trying out your own rejection therapy. Here's a quick and easy guide to get you started on it.

The first step to know about rejection therapy is that the goal is to get rejected. This means that as you approach strangers and ask them for things, you can't ask them for something that is within the realm of possibility, else wise they might say yes. So if you ask someone to borrow their phone to make a quick call, they might be willing to let you use it, but if you asked them to borrow 100 bucks, they would be far more reticent.

The plan is to expose yourself to as much rejection as possible, that way you are able to experience the emotional pain of rejection in a safe manner. So don't make requests of people that you know, strangers would be far better because they are far more likely to refuse your request. Try to make a habit of asking a stranger of something bizarre or outlandish about once a week for a few months and see how it affects you. This is a great way to develop a resistance to the fear of being rejected.

The more you do this, the better you will become at making requests and the better you will be at being rejected. Now, this might seem absurd, but don't take my word for it. Give it a try and see how you feel after the fifth or sixth time that you've been rejected. Chances are it will improve your ability to process and handle rejection from other people and in the process it will make you become a boss!

Confidence Factor Six: Have Goals

The final piece to the confidence puzzle is learning how to develop goals for yourself. The reason that most confident people appear to get so much done is because they have a system of developing goals that allow them to be constantly moving forward. You see, when you don't have goals, you will have nothing to strive towards. Your confidence level will naturally lower or rise based on the amount of effort and energy you are using to reach these goals. If you have no goals, then guess what? You won't be a particularly confident individual.

Why are goals and confidence so closely linked? Well, it's because confidence is based off of the ability to *achieve* something. A person who is confident believes that they are able to get specific things done. How can you be confident if there is nothing to achieve? This step often gets overlooked when it comes to learning to be more confident because it is action-oriented, but actions are a necessary component to being a confident person. No one is ever confident just because. Rather, they are confident because they have the necessary tools to achieve whatever they wish to achieve in this life.

Do you have goals? If not, then you would do well to sit down and start writing up what your goals are. They can be short term goals or long term, it doesn't really matter. All that matters is that your goals are sufficiently able to motivate you to achieve them. The more motivated you are, the more confident you will become. Someone who lacks motivation will rarely ever have confidence.

Goal setting should be a regular part of your life if you want to become a boss. The easiest way to set goals is to use a system known a SMART, which is an acronym that means:

Specific:

- You must ask yourself what you are trying to achieve it.
- It should be highly specific to what you are trying to accomplish.
- Example: I want to learn how to speak publicly

Measurable

- A measurable means the results that you are looking for.
- It can be based on quantity or some kind of accomplishment
- Example: I want to be able to give a best man's speech without freezing up.

Attainable

- You must then figure out how you want to achieve your goal
- It is based on your own skills, not other people's
- Example: I am going to memorize the speech and practice it in the mirror 100 times.

Realistic

- This part is simply measuring what your goals are and your methods and making sure that they are realistic
- Example: 100 times seems an awful lot and I have a full-time job, since the wedding is next month, that isn't realistic. I'll adjust it to 15 times.

Time Based

- This part is the deadline for when you will have your goal met
- Example: I will have it met by August 15th, 2018.

By using the SMART goal system, you will easily be able to set up goals and then follow through with them on a daily, weekly or monthly basis.

Chapter 4: Conclusion

Well, that about does it for our discussion on what it means to become a boss! Remember, a boss is very different from a manager, because a manager's power comes from the external sources of control that he has. Things like position, coercion and the power to bribe can vanish in an instant, and then what are you left with?

When you become a boss, no matter what circumstances change around you, your own power and influence over people won't sway with the wind. When you root yourself to the principles of true leadership, connection, influence and confidence, you will become like the mighty oak tree, planted with deep roots. No matter what may happen in your life, if you work on these principles, nothing will be able to topple you. Don't just be a manager, be a boss and live the kind of life that people from all around will point at and say "now that's the kind of person I will follow!" It's not an easy life to live, it takes sacrifice, hard work and the ability to care about people who aren't you, but if you can follow these principles, you will find a life that is satisfying beyond all reason. And people will know that you are the ultimate boss.

Other books available by Landon T. Smith on Kindle, paperback and audio:

Why NLP Isn't Working For You

The Art of Influence

The Power of Reflection: Embrace Your Past to Find a Purpose for Your Future

Meet Maslow: How Understanding the Priorities of Those Around Us Can Lead to Harmony and Improvement

Manderstanding: Learn How to Read the Cues and Understand the Motives of the Male Gender

Deconstruction Of Self: Untangling Negative Thoughts About Yourself To Rebuild A Self Of Steel

The End of Chaos: Break Away From Bad Habits, Addictions and Self Destructive Tendencies Before They Break You

www.ingramcontent.com/pod-product-compliance
Lightning Source LLC
Chambersburg PA
CBHW030904180526
45163CB00004B/1701